10
12
15
Gt.
17
Pos. mf
Reduce Ped. -32', Large Reeds

19
♩ = 69
23
27
31
stringendo
Gt.
- Sw. Reeds
f

from "Prelude in G Major," BWV 625 - J. S. Bach

♩ = 76

42
45
47
50